Theory Paper   Grade 1   2019   A
Model Answers

1

(a)

(b)

2   C major   G major   F major   (10)

G major   F major   D major

3   (10)

4 (a)   (10)

(b)   —Abrsm made a mistake!

5   (10)

6  (10)

7 (a) D D F# E A C# B G D (10)

  (b) six

8 (10)

p means:

very quiet	☐
loud	☐
very loud	☐
quiet	✔

—— means:

gradually getting louder	✔
gradually getting quicker	☐
accent the note	☐
loud	☐

cantabile means:

smoothly	☐
in a singing style	✔
at a medium speed	☐
gradually getting quieter	☐

Lento means:

smoothly	☐
at a medium speed	☐
very slow	☐
slow	✔

 means:

tie: detached	☐
slur: perform smoothly	☐
slur: detached	☐
tie: hold for the value of both notes	✔

Fine means:

in time	☐
a little	☐
the end	✔
repeat from the beginning	☐

9 (a) (i) two (10)

  (ii) semibreve / whole note

  (iii) C

  (iv) 6

  (v) *staccato* (detached)

  (b) (10)

  cresc.   *f*   dim.   *mf*

4

Theory Paper   Grade 1   2019   B
Model Answers

1 (10)

2 (10)

(a)

(b)   D F♯ A   C E G

3 (10)

4   6th   8th / 8ve   2nd   (10)

3rd   7th   4th

5 (10)

6 (a) 3rd   4th   2nd   6th   7th   8th / 8ve / 1st   5th   3rd   1st / 8th / 8ve   (10)

(b) dotted minim / dotted half note

7   𝅝   𝅗𝅥   𝅗𝅥.   𝅘𝅥   𝅘𝅥𝅮   𝅘𝅥𝅯   (10)

8 (10)

poco means:		*legato* means:		*pp* means:	
detached	☐	smoothly	✔	very loud	☐
in time	☐	very quiet	☐	moderately loud	☐
a little	✔	gradually getting slower	☐	moderately quiet	☐
the end	☐	detached	☐	very quiet	✔

ritenuto means:		*diminuendo* means:		**Allegro** means:	
gradually getting quicker	☐	gradually getting quieter	✔	fairly quick	☐
slow	☐	gradually getting louder	☐	quick	✔
held back	✔	gradually getting quicker	☐	at a medium speed	☐
gradually getting slower	☐	quiet	☐	slow	☐

9 (a) (10)

(i)   Bar 3 / 7

(ii)   3

(iii)   B♭

(iv)   false

      false

(b) (10)

Adagio   *p cantabile*   *mp*

Music Theory Practice Papers 2019

Model Answers

ABRSM Grade 1

Welcome to ABRSM's *Music Theory Practice Papers 2019 Model Answers*, Grade 1. These answers are a useful resource for students and teachers preparing for ABRSM theory exams and should be used alongside the relevant published theory practice papers.

For more information on how theory papers are marked and some general advice on taking theory exams, please refer to **www.abrsm.org/theory**.

Using these answers

- Answers are given in the same order and, where possible, in the same layout as in the exam papers, making it easy to match answer to question.

- Where it is necessary to show the answer on a stave, the original stave is printed in grey with the answer shown in black, for example:

- Alternative answers are separated by an oblique stroke (/) or by *or*, for example:

    getting slower / gradually getting slower

- The old-style crotchet rest is accepted as a valid alternative to the modern symbol .

- Answers that require the candidate to write out a scale or chord have been shown at one octave only. Reasonable alternatives at different octaves can also receive full marks.

- Sometimes the clef, key and time signature of the relevant bar(s) are included for added clarity, for example:

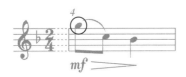

© 2020 by The Associated Board of the Royal Schools of Music
Published by ABRSM (Publishing) Ltd, a wholly owned subsidiary of ABRSM
Cover by Kate Benjamin & Andy Potts
Printed in England by Halstan & Co. Ltd, Amersham, Bucks., on materials from sustainable sources

Theory Paper   Grade 1   2019   C
Model Answers

1 (a)   (10)

(b)

2   *ff*   *f*   *mf*   *mp*   *p*   *pp*   (10)

3 (a) 1st   3rd   5th   6th   7th   8th /   4th   2nd   1st /   (10)
                                                            8ve / 1st   8th / 8ve

(b) eight

4   (10)

Key C major

Key F major

Key G major

5   (10)

(a)

(b)   F A C   D F♯ A

7

6 (10)

7 (10)

8 (10)

crescendo means:

gradually getting quieter	☐
gradually getting louder	☑
loud	☐
quick	☐

mf means:

quiet	☐
very loud	☐
moderately loud	☑
moderately quiet	☐

rall. means:

gradually getting slower	☑
held back	☐
slow	☐
gradually getting quicker	☐

Allegro moderato means:

moderately loud	☐
moderately quiet	☐
moderately slow	☐
moderately quick	☑

◌̇ means:

staccato: smoothly	☐
staccato: detached	☑
accent the note	☐
legato: detached	☐

dal segno (D.S.) means:

repeat from the sign 𝄋	☑
the end	☐
repeat from the beginning	☐
in time	☐

9 (a) (10)

    (i)   Bar 3

    (ii)   two

    (iii)   D

    (iv)   true

         true

  (b) (10)

Allegro ♩ = 100

f

Theory Paper   Grade 1   2019   S
Model Answers

1   (10)

2   (10)

3 (a) E   C   A   F   E   B   G   D   C   (10)

  (b) two

4   (10)

5   7th   6th   3rd   (10)
          2nd   4th   8th / 8ve

6 G major   F major   C major   (10)

F major   C major   D major

7 (a)   (10)

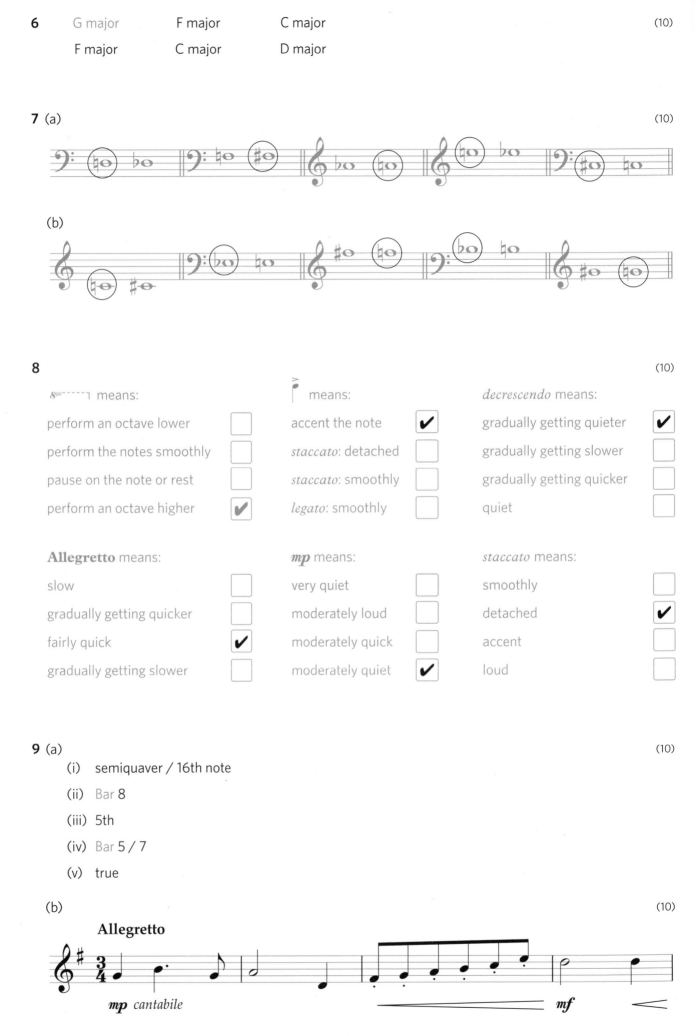

(b)

8   (10)

$8^{va}\ulcorner\cdots\urcorner$ means:

perform an octave lower	☐
perform the notes smoothly	☐
pause on the note or rest	☐
perform an octave higher	✔

$\overset{>}{\bullet}$ means:

accent the note	✔
staccato: detached	☐
staccato: smoothly	☐
legato: smoothly	☐

decrescendo means:

gradually getting quieter	✔
gradually getting slower	☐
gradually getting quicker	☐
quiet	☐

Allegretto means:

slow	☐
gradually getting quicker	☐
fairly quick	✔
gradually getting slower	☐

mp means:

very quiet	☐
moderately loud	☐
moderately quick	☐
moderately quiet	✔

staccato means:

smoothly	☐
detached	✔
accent	☐
loud	☐

9 (a)   (10)

(i)   semiquaver / 16th note

(ii) Bar 8

(iii) 5th

(iv) Bar 5 / 7

(v)   true

(b)   (10)